Contents

T0352612

These super-sized scenes act as a wonderful focal point for your class. Look for objects that contain the featured target sound. You may like to introduce a fuller vocabulary using words from the list at the bottom of each page.

 Clever Cat loves watching Kicking King kick at the end of words.

 kick

 sock

duck

sack

truck

Extra vocabulary to find in the scene:
black, bucket, chicks, dock, muck, rocket, rucksack, ticket, track

 When Noisy Nick and Golden Girl meet, they si**ng** a special 'ng' song.

sing

king

painting

wing

ring

Extra vocabulary to find in the scene: dripping, eating, flying, hang, Kicking King, painting, reading, ring, running, sing, sitting, sliding

3

ch

When Clever Cat is next to Harry, his hairy hat makes her sneeze, "ch!"

 chin  chair   chicken  peaches  children

Extra vocabulary to find in the scene: chain, chart, cheese, cherries, chest, chicken, chicks, chime, chilli, Chinese food, chocolate, chop, kitchen

 **sh** Harry Hat Man says "sh!" to hush Sammy Snake up.

 shop

 ship

shell

 fish

 shoe

Extra vocabulary to find in the scene: mushroom, push, radish, shades, shadow, shapes, shark, shed, sheep, shepherd, shoes, shore, shrimp, sunshine

th Talking Tess and Harry Hat Man **th**ink the **th**under is too loud.

throw

thank you

three

bath

path

Extra vocabulary to find in the scene: athlete, birthday card, length, month, mouthwash, Southport, thatched, theatre, thimble, thistle, thorns, thread

Harry Hat Man takes Peter Puppy's **ph**oto.

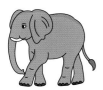 elephant  telephone  dolphin  photograph alphabet

Extra vocabulary to find in the scene: bibliography, digraphs, graph, pamphlet, pharaoh, pheasant, phonics, photographer, physics, sapphire, trophy

  Walter Walrus **wh**ooshes Harry Hat Man's hat off so Harry is too startled to speak.

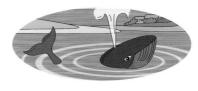

wheel **wheat** **whale** **white** **whistle**

Extra vocabulary to find in the scene: wheeled bin, whelk, whippet, whirlpool, whiskers, Whitley Bay, whittle

 **a_e** This Magic **e** you cannot hear has the power to make a Vowel Man appear.

 gate    cake    grapes   lake    skate

Extra vocabulary to find in the scene: cape, cave, crate, face, game, lane, page, plane, race, rake, snake, snowflakes, spade, wave

When two vowels go out walking,
the first one does the talking.

 rain

 snail

 chain

 paint

 train

Extra vocabulary to find in the scene: daisy chain, drain, grain, hail, mail, paid, railway, raincoat, raisins, sail, sailor, snail trail, waiter, wait, waiting room

 **ay** When two vowels go out walking, the first one does the talking.

	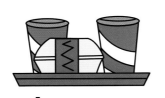			
spray	takeaway	holiday	tray	play

Extra vocabulary to find in the scene: airways, birthday, Caymans, delay, Friday, getaway, Norway, Malaysia, May, runway, stairway, subway, today, x-ray

 This Magic e you cannot hear has the power to make a Vowel Man appear.

 complete

 delete

 scene

 compete

 athlete

Extra vocabulary to find in the scene:
centipede, concrete, Irene, Steve, millipede, Pete, theme park

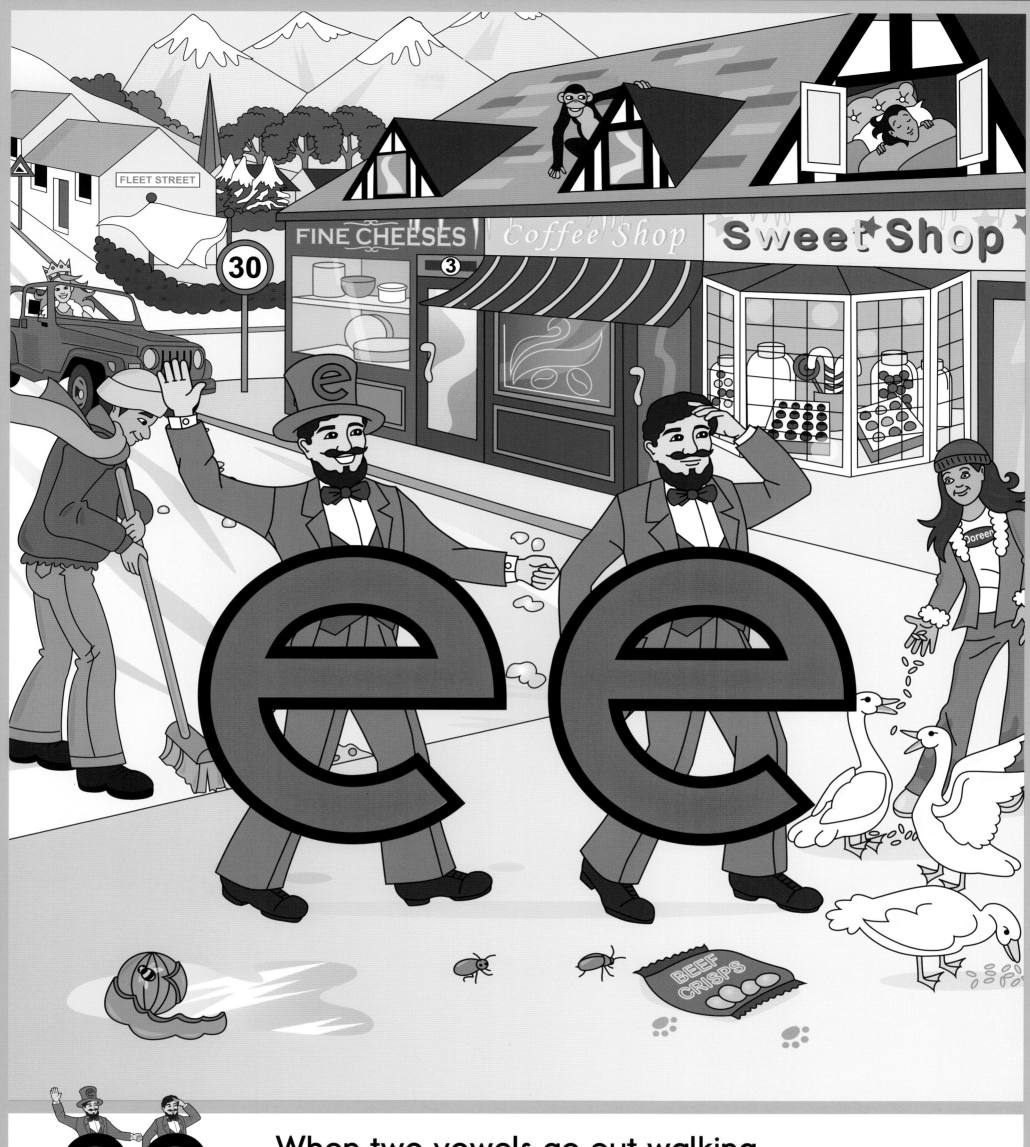

 When two vowels go out walking,
the first one does the talking.

tree

cheese

jeep

sleep

sweep

Extra vocabulary: asleep, bee, beef crisps, beetle, breeze, cheese, chimpanzee, coffee, feed, fleece, Fleet Street, freezing, geese, green, peel, queen, steeple

 When two vowels go out walking,
the first one does the talking.

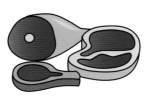 peach

 meat

peas

 tea

 leaf

Extra vocabulary to find in the scene: beads, beans, beat, cheap, cleaning, cream, deals, eat, jeans, leaves, peas, seafood, seal, tea, yeast

Yellow Yo-yo Man works for Mr E
in many, many words.

family

party

puppy

teddy

story

Extra vocabulary to find in the scene: berry, Bouncy Ben, bunny, Dippy Duck, dummy, fairy, frosty, holly, ivy, misty, Vicky Violet

 This Magic e you cannot hear has the power to make a Vowel Man appear.

slide

kite

bike

lime

mice

Extra vocabulary to find in the scene: five, hide, hive, ice, knife, nice, nine, pine, ride, smile, stripes, sunshine, white, vines

 When these two vowels go out walking,
Mr I usually does the talking.

pie	flies	tie	fries	magpie

Extra vocabulary to find in the scene:
died (tree), fries, magnified, magpie

 igh When Mr I stands next to Golden Girl he gives her an ice cream for being quiet.

 light

 night

 fight

 right

bright

Extra vocabulary to find in the scene:
flight, fright, high, knight, midnight, moonlight, spotlight

 Sometimes Yellow Yo-yo Man says "i" for Mr I.

 fly

 cry

sky

 July

 why

Extra vocabulary to find in the scene:
dry (washing), shy, spy, magnify, multiply

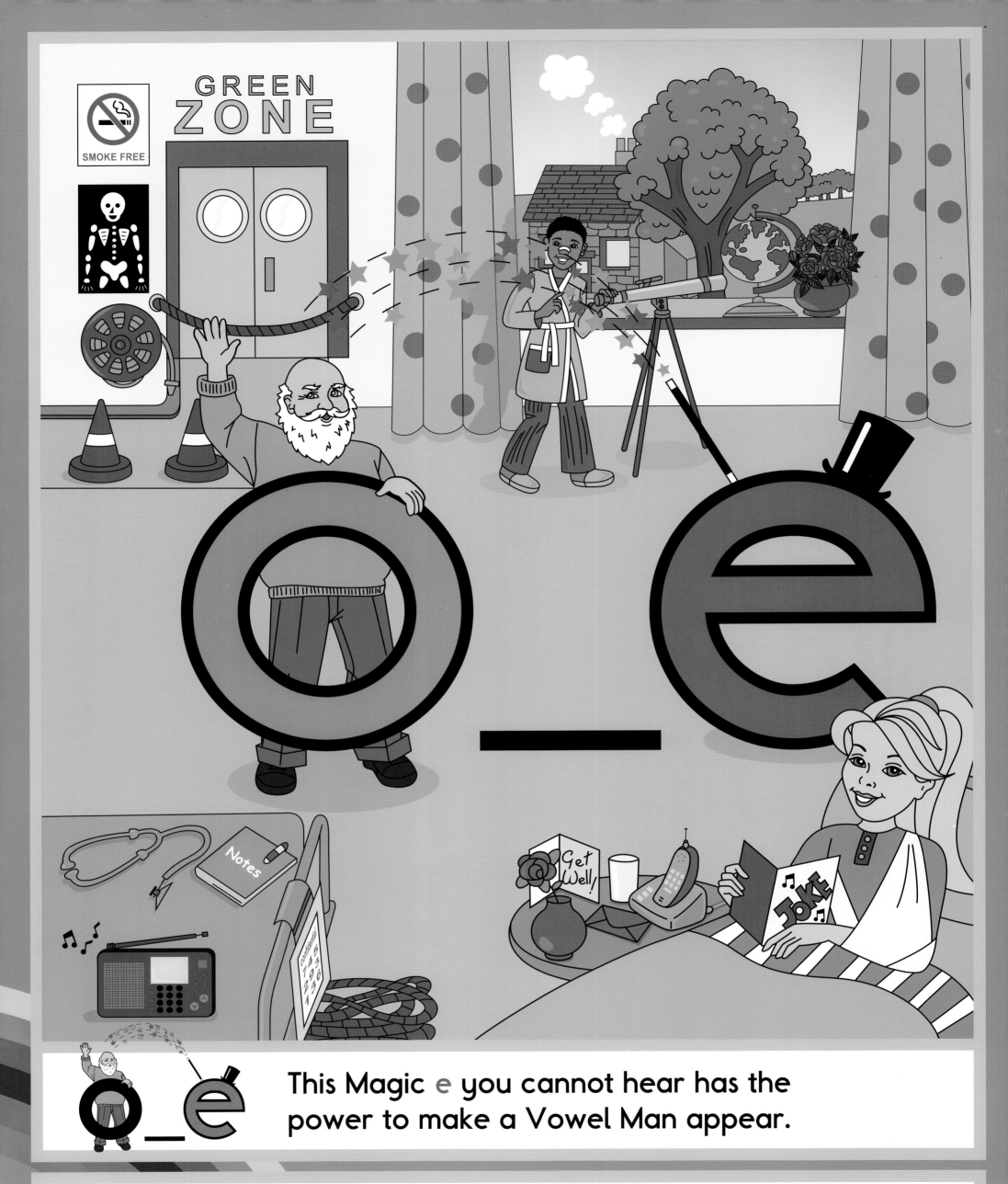

 This Magic **e** you cannot hear has the power to make a Vowel Man appear.

 rose phone nose  rope  smoke

Extra vocabulary to find in the scene: bone, code, cone, globe, home, hose, joke, notes, robe, stone, stethoscope, telescope, zone

 When two vowels go out walking,
the first one does the talking.

 boat

 goat

 soap

 goal

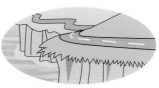 road

Extra vocabulary to find in the scene: *coach, coal, coast, coat, float, foal, foam, load, loaf, moat, oak, oats, poached, road, soak, stoat, toad, toast*

 Mr O surprises Walter by shouting out his last name, "O".

 yellow

 window

 snow

elbow

 bowl

Extra vocabulary to find in the scene: arrow, blow, bungalow, bow, bowls, burrow, crow, flow, marrow, meadow, mow, rows, scarecrow, sparrow, swallow

u_e This Magic **e** you cannot hear has the power to make a Vowel Man appear.

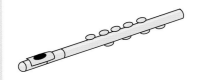 flute

 cube

 parachute

 tube

 perfume

Extra vocabulary to find in the scene:
computer, costume, dunes, June, tunes

NOTE: Depending on accent, sometimes **u_e** sounds like 'oo', and other times it sounds like '**you**'.

ue

 **ue**

When two vowels go out walking,
the first one does the talking.

 blue

 Tuesday

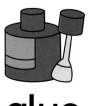 barbecue

glue

 argue

NOTE: Depending on accent, sometimes **ue** sounds like 'oo', and other times it sounds like '**you**'.

Extra vocabulary to find in the scene:
avenue, bluebells, clue, fuel, fondue, muesli, rescue, tissue, value, venue

 The Boot Twin says "Oo, I have your boots".

 zoo

 boot

 spoon

 balloon

 food

Extra vocabulary to find in the scene: baboon, bamboo, broom, cockatoo, goose, hoop, igloo, kangaroo, macaroon, moon, moose, racoon, stool, tools

When Eddy Elephant squirts Walter Walrus with water, Walter cries, "Oo! You!"

 news

 jewels

 cashews

 stew

 chew

NOTE: Depending on accent, sometimes **ew** sounds like **'oo'**, and other times it sounds like **'you'**.

Extra vocabulary to find in the scene: crew, ewe, flew, interview, new potatoes, preview, screws, shrew, steward, view, yew tree

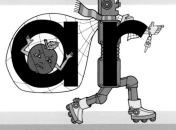 **Arthur Ar** steals apples and reports back with his last name, "Ar!"

 stars

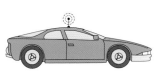 car

 scarf

 card

 farmyard

Extra vocabulary to find in the scene: archery board, alarm, armadillo, bark, barn, cart, carve/carving, chart, dark, farmer, guitar, postcards, varnish

 Orvil Or steals oranges and reports back with his last name, "Or!"

 **horse**

 **fork**

 **storm**

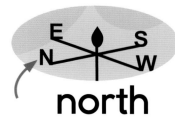 **north**

 **sport**

Extra vocabulary to find in the scene: acorn, corn, corner, horns, orchard, orchids, porcupine, sports, score, shore, stork, shorts, tornado

 Ernest Er steals elephants and reports back with his last name, "Er!"

 tiger

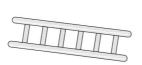 danger

ladder

 hammer

 painter

Extra vocabulary to find in the scene: anteater, badger, beaver, butterfly, carpenter, cleaner, fern, flowers, helicopter, otter, panther, ranger, spider, water

29

 Irving Ir steals ink and reports back with his last name, "Ir!"

bird

shirt

birthday

skirt

girl

Extra vocabulary to find in the scene: birch, birthday cake, circus, dirty, girder, headfirst, fir cones, fir trees, ladybird, sirloin steak, squirt, swirl, twirl

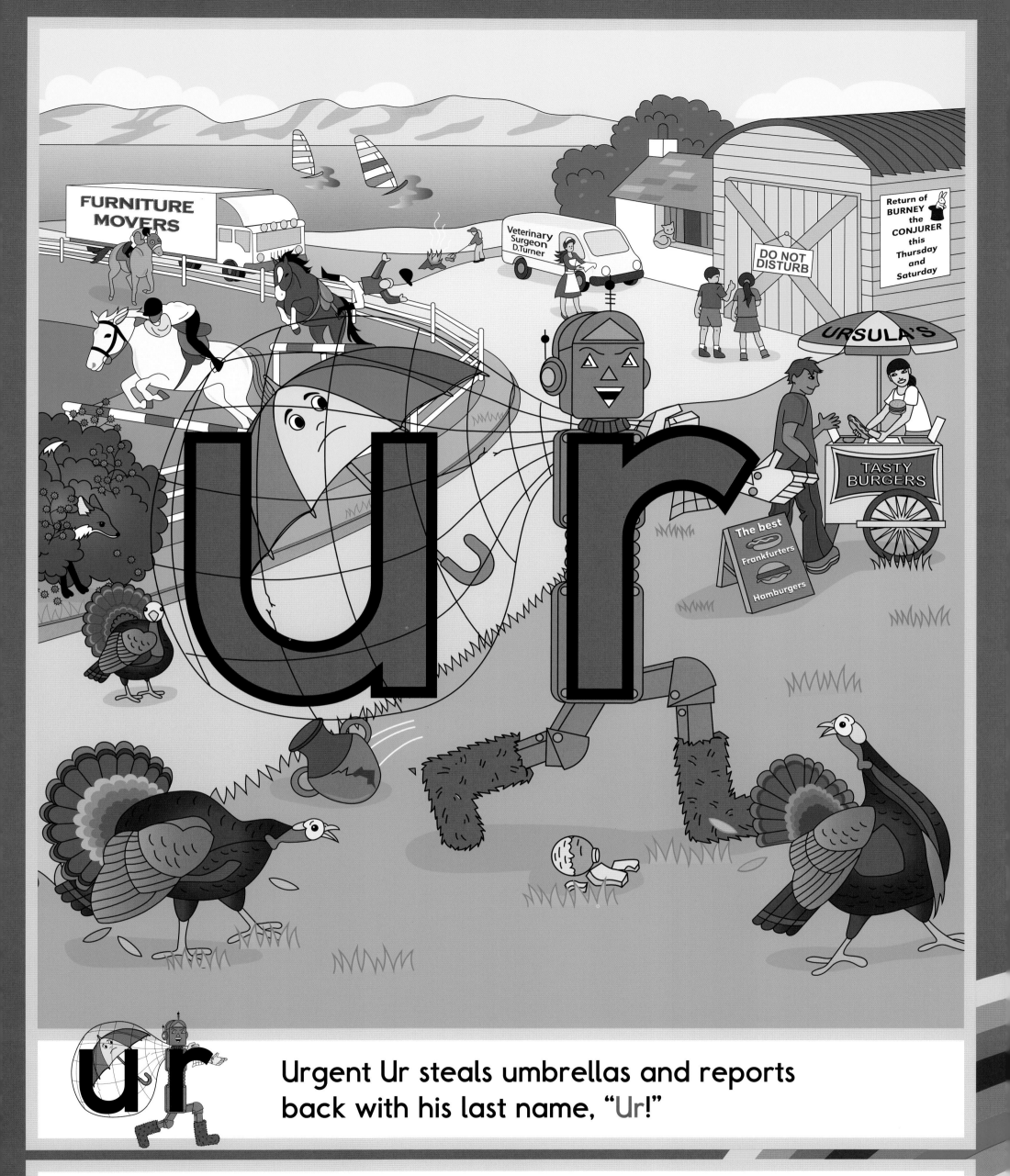

 **ur** Urgent Ur steals umbrellas and reports back with his last name, "Ur!"

 nurse

 purse

 burger

 fur

 purple

Extra vocabulary to find in the scene: burn, conjurer, curb, curl, curtain, frankfurters, furniture, hurdles, Saturday, surgery, Thursday, turkey, turnip

Write your message here!

GIFT SHOP

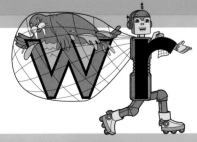

Red Robot captures Walter in his sack.
Walter is too startled to speak.

write

wriggle

wreck

wrapper

wring

Extra vocabulary to find in the scene: typewriter, wreath, wren, wrench, wrestling, wrinkles, wristwatch, writhe, wrong, wrought iron

Claire's Hair Salon

Hair Spray

Dairy

air

When a Robot captures Mr A and Mr I it puffs out "air".

 fair

 hair

 chair

 stairs

 fairy

Extra vocabulary to find in the scene:
air, Claire, dairy, eclairs, hairspray, hairdryer, pair of scissors

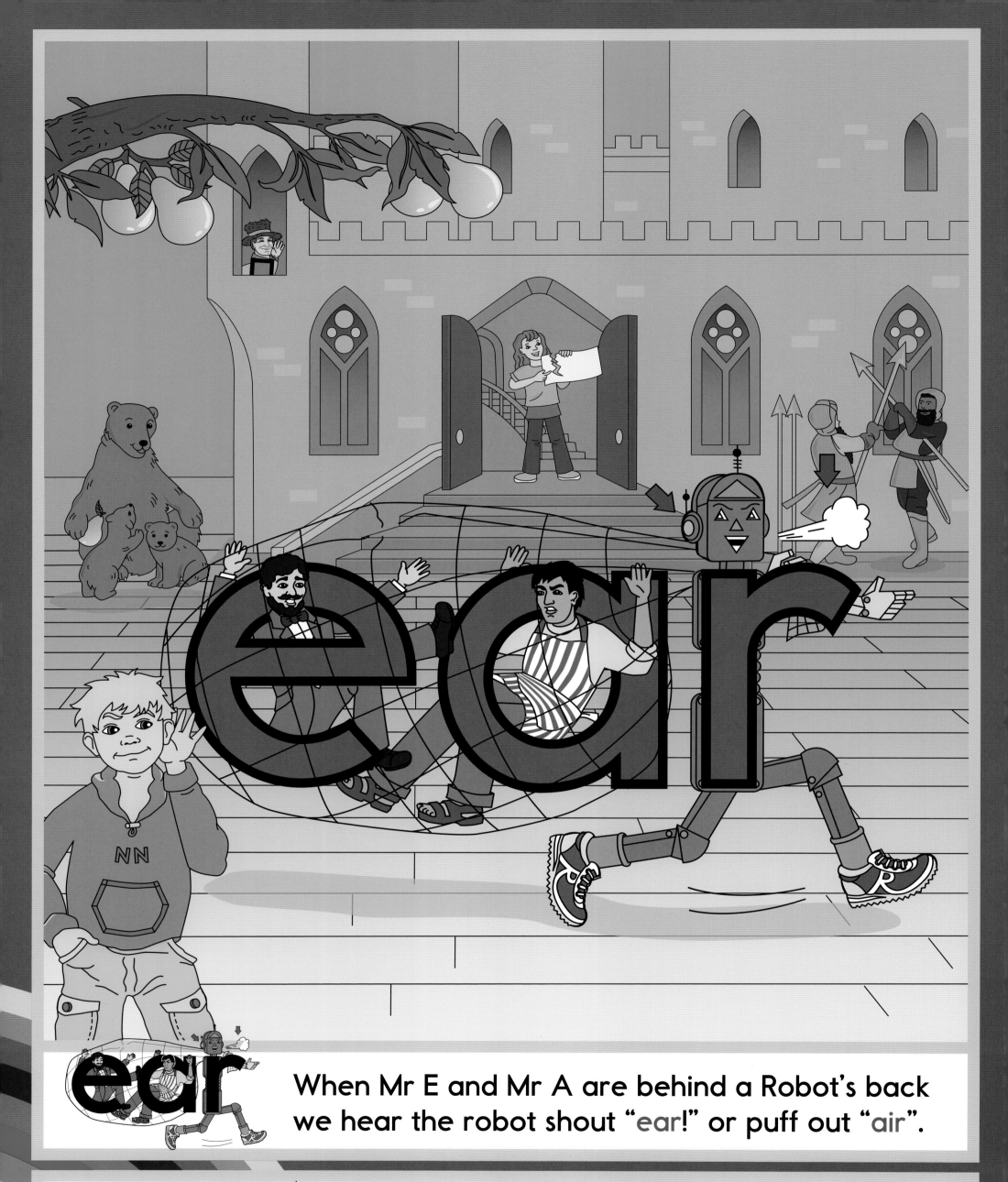

 When Mr E and Mr A are behind a Robot's back we hear the robot shout "ear!" or puff out "air".

 hear

spear

 ear

 pear

 tear

 bear

Extra vocabulary to find in the scene:
appear, beard, clear, near

Oscar Orange's Bothersome Little Brother can't say "o" like Oscar. Instead he just says "uh".

 monkey

 money

 son

 dove

 honey

 The Foot Twin says "Oo, just look at my foot!"

 foot    wood    book    hood    wool

Extra vocabulary to find in the scene:
cookbook, cookies, cooker, football, hook, woof

BAKERY

Butcher

CAFÉ

③

PULL

PUSH

Lots of puddings!

 Umbrellas that are pushed and pulled into letters don't make their usual sound.

push

pull

bull

sugar

cushion

Extra vocabulary to find in the scene:
butcher, bush, cuckoo, full, Giant Full, pudding, pussy cat

 **oy**

Roy plays the 'Oy game' at the end of words.

toys   boy   destroy   annoyed   soy

Extra vocabulary to find in the scene:
corduroy, cowboy hat, gargoyle (mask), royal, voyage

Roy plays the 'Oi game' inside words.

boil **oil** **soil** **coins** **noise**

Extra vocabulary to find in the scene: boiler, coil, foil, joints (elbows and knees), ointment, point (Mr I) poison, sirloin, toilet (roll)

 When Walter Walrus splashes Annie Apple she cries "Aw! Don't be so awful!".

 jigsaw

 yawn

 straw

 paw

 saw

Extra vocabulary to find in the scene:
coleslaw, dawn, fawn, hawk, seesaw, shawl, strawberries, straws, trawler, yawn

 Walter Walrus hides in Uppy Umbrella's letter and splashes Annie Apple. She cries "Au! Don't be so awful!".

 autumn

 astronaut

 saucer

 launch

 caution

Extra vocabulary to find in the scene: applaud, auburn, author, autobiography, autograph, caution, Claude, haunted house, laundry, nautical, tarpaulin (tent)

 Walter Walrus bumps his chin as he splashes Oscar Orange. They both howl, "Ow!"

 vowels

 cow

 town

 towels

 shower

Extra vocabulary to find in the scene: brown, clown, crowd, eyebrow, flowers, frown, gown, talcum powder, tower, trowel, owls

 Walter Walrus bumps his chin as he splashes Oscar Orange. They both shout, "Ou!"

 mountain

 fountain

 clouds

 mouse

 house

Extra vocabulary to find in the scene: bounce, found, ground, hound, loud, outside, pound, pounce, round, sound, scout, trousers

Clever Cat as a hissing snake.

 **face**  **space**  **city** **circle**  **bicycle**  **cylinder**

Extra vocabulary to find in the scene: ambulance, accident, December, entrance, fence, finance, ice pack, medicine, pencil, pharmacy, recycling, science

gé gi gy

Gentle Ginger the gymnast.

vegetables

orange

giraffe

gym

gymnast

Extra vocabulary to find in the scene: danger, energy gel, fringe, gentlemen, ginger, gymnastics, hygiene gel, magic wand, Manager's Office, pages, tangerine

 Noisy Nick has a **kn**ack of getting in the way of Kicking King's kicks. The king is too angry to speak.

 knit

 knight

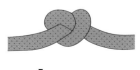 knot

 knock

 knife

Extra vocabulary to find in the scene: door knob, door knocker, knapsack, knee, kneeling, knickers, knitting needle, knowledge, knuckle

← School Archive

Choir
Choral Chords at Christmas

School Orchestra
Christmas Concert

Technology in Chemistry

Christine Nichols

Aches
Headache
Stomach ache

Understanding the Chemistry

Chemical

Chlorine

Echoes
Chemistry

 When the wind blows off Harry Hat Man's hat, Clever Cat makes her usual 'c' sound.

 school    choir   mechanic    chemical    orchestra

Extra vocabulary to find in the scene: ache, anchor (t-shirt), architect, characters, chemist, chlorine, choral, chords, Christmas, chrome (table), echoes, orchid, technology

 Mr Mean-E says, "Hee, hee, hee, I'm an e, but I say 'a...' in words like th**e**y".

 grey

 prey

 8 eight

 freight

 sleigh

Extra vocabulary to find in the scene:
abseil, beige, disobey, neigh, obey, osprey, reins, reindeer, survey, weight

+ addition
- subtraction
x multiplication

 **tion** Mr 'Tion's trick is to remember the phrase "Tea I Owe Nick".

 caution  portion  dictionary   addition subtraction

Extra vocabulary to find in the scene: action, construction, correction, exhibition, exploration, fiction, fraction, introduction, multiplication, section

 Talking Tess always sneezes next to Urgent Ur at the end of a word.

 picture

 sculpture

 vulture

 furniture

 puncture

Extra vocabulary to find in the scene: adventure, architecture, creature, culture, departure, future, gesture (wave), literature, mixture, nature, pasture, picture

Ball stall

3 for 2 small balls

all

When you see Giant All's long legs next to an apple, the apple won't make its usual sound.

 ball

 fall

 wall

 holdall

 stall

Extra vocabulary to find in the scene:
call, small, tall, waterfall

 **ful**

Giant Full sometimes pulls a word up beside him and leans on it. Then we can only see one of his legs.

 **mouthful**

 **handful**

 **armful**

 **spoonful**

 **playful**

Extra vocabulary to find in the scene: basketful, bowlful, bucketful, colourful, cupful, mouthful, painful, plateful, playful, restful

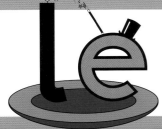 Candle Magic changes Lucy into a Magic candle.

 table  stable  apple bottle  puzzle

Extra vocabulary to find in the scene: beetle, bridle, castle, drizzle, eagle, fables, giggle, huddle, hurdle, kettle, little, marbles, maple, noodles, puddle, wobble, thistle

 This Magic ing Ending is just as powerful as Silent Magic e and Magic ed.

 driving

 racing

skating

 riding

 smoking

 skating

Extra vocabulary to find in the scene: baking, driving, exciting, fading (light), parachuting, racing, roller-skating, shining, smiling

éd éd éd

Eddy Elephant and Dippy Duck sound like 'ed', 'd' or 't'.

spotted invited

phoned saved

snapped stroked

Extra vocabulary to find in the scene:
faded (umbrella), lined (paper), seated (man), smiled (girl), skated

Spelling Stories

Spelling	Spelling Story
ck	Clever Cat loves watching Ki**ck**ing King ki**ck** at the end of words.
ng	When Noisy Nick and Golden Girl meet, they si**ng** a special '**ng**' so**ng**.
ch	When Clever Cat is next to Harry, his hairy hat makes her sneeze, "**ch**!"
sh	Harry Hat Man says "**sh**!" to hu**sh** Sammy Snake up.
th	Talking Tess and Harry Hat Man **th**ink the **th**under is too loud.
ph	Harry Hat Man takes Peter Puppy's **ph**oto.
wh	Walter Walrus **wh**ooshes Harry Hat Man's hat off so Harry is too startled to speak.
a_e	This Magic **e** you cannot hear has the power to make a Vowel Man appear.
ai	When two vowels go out walking, the first one does the talking.
ay	When two vowels go out walking, the first one does the talking.

Spelling	Spelling Story
e_e	This Magic **e** you cannot hear has the power to make a Vowel Man appear.
ee	When two vowels go out walking, the first one does the talking.
ea	When two vowels go out walking, the first one does the talking.
y	Yellow Yo-yo Man works for Mr E in man**y**, man**y** words.
i_e	This Magic **e** you cannot hear has the power to make a Vowel Man appear.
ie	When these two vowels go out walking, Mr I usually does the talking.
igh	When Mr I stands next to Golden Girl, he gives her an ice cream for being quiet.
y	Sometimes Yellow Yo-yo Man says "**i**" for Mr I.
o_e	This Magic **e** you cannot hear has the power to make a Vowel Man appear.
oa	When two vowels go out walking, the first one does the talking.

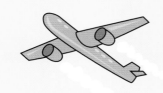

Spelling	Spelling Story
ow	Mr O surprises Walter by shouting out his last name, "**O**".
u_e	This Magic **e** you cannot hear has the power to make a Vowel Man appear.
ue	When two vowels go out walking, the first one does the talking.
oo	The Boot Twin says "**Oo**, I have your b**oo**ts".
ew	When Eddy Elephant squirts Walter Walrus with water, Walter cries, "**Oo! You!**"
ar	Arthur Ar steals apples and reports back with his last name, "**Ar!**"
or	Orvil Or steals oranges and reports back with his last name, "**Or!**"
er	Ernest Er steals elephants and reports back with his last name, "**Er!**"
ir	Irving Ir steals ink and reports back with his last name, "**Ir!**"
ur	Urgent Ur steals umbrellas and reports back with his last name, "**Ur!**"

Spelling	Spelling Story
wr	Red Robot captures Walter in his sack. Walter is too startled to speak.
air	When a Robot captures Mr A and Mr I, it puffs out "**air**".
ear **ear**	When Mr E and Mr A are behind a Robot's back we hear the robot shout "**ear!**" or puff out "**air**".
o	Oscar Orange's Bothersome Little Brother can't say 'o' like Oscar. Instead he just says, '**uh**'.
oo	The Foot Twin says "**Oo**, just look at my f**oo**t!"
u	Umbrellas that are p**u**shed and p**u**lled into letters don't make their usual sound.
oy	Roy plays the '**Oy** game' at the end of words.
oi	Roy plays the '**Oi** game' inside words.
aw	When Walter Walrus splashes Annie Apple she cries "**Aw!** Don't be so **aw**ful!".

Spelling	Spelling Story	Spelling	Spelling Story
au	Walter Walrus hides in Uppy Umbrella's letter and splashes Annie Apple. She cries "**Au**! Don't be so awful!".	**e**	Mr Mean-E says, "Hee, hee, hee, I'm an e, but I say '**a**...' in words like th**ey**".
ow	Walter Walrus bumps his chin as he splashes Oscar Orange. They both h**ow**l, "**Ow**!"	**tion**	Mr 'Tion's trick is to remember the phrase "Tea I Owe Nick".
ou	Walter Walrus bumps his chin as he splashes Oscar Orange. They both howl, "**Ou**!"	**ture**	Talking Tess makes her usual sound beside Red Robot.
ce	Clever Cat as a hissing snake.	**all**	When you see Giant All's long legs next to an apple, the apple won't make its usual sound.
ci		**ful**	Giant Full sometimes pulls a word up beside him and leans on it. Then we can only see one of his legs.
cy		**le**	Candle Magic changes Lucy into a Magic cand**le**.
ge	Gentle Ginger the gymnast.	**ing**	This Magic Ending is just as powerful as Silent Magic e and Magic ed.
gi		**ed**	Eddy Elephant and Dippy Duck sound like '**ed**', '**d**' or '**t**'.
gy		**ed**	
kn	Noisy Nick has a **kn**ack of getting in the way of Kicking King's kicks. The king is too angry to speak.	**ed**	
ch	When the wind blows off Harry Hat Man's hat, Clever Cat makes her usual 'c' sound.		

Long Vowels

When you hear a Vowel Man's name in a word, look for a way to spell it here.

 **a**    **a_e**    **ai**    **ay**

 **e**    **e_e**    **ee**    **ea**    **y**

 **i**    **i_e**    **ie**    **igh**    **y**

 **o**    **o_e**    **oa**    **ow**

 **u**    **u_e**    **ue**    **oo**    **ew**

The Vowel Stealers

Be careful when you see this band of Vowel Stealing Robots!
They capture vowels so they can't make their usual sounds.

Reading Direction